In the Village of the Elephants

JEREMY SCHMIDT   photographs by TED WOOD

WALKER AND COMPANY   New York

First published in the United States of America in 1994 by
Walker Publishing Company, Inc.

Published simultaneously in Canada by
Thomas Allen & Son Canada, Limited, Markham, Ontario

Library of Congress Cataloging-in-Publication Data
Schmidt, Jeremy.
In the village of the elephants / Jeremy Schmidt : photographs by
Ted Wood.
p.   cm.
Includes bibliographical references and index.
ISBN 0-8027-8226-4.—ISBN 0-8027-8227-2 (lib. bdg.)
1. Elephants—India—Nilgiri Hills—Juvenile literature.
2. Nilgiri Hills (India)—Social life and customs—Juvenile
literature. [1. Elephants. 2. India—Social life and customs.]
I. Wood, Ted, 1965– ill. II. Title.
QL737.P98S37   1994
636′ .961′0954—dc20   93-8545
CIP
AC

Printed in Hong Kong

2 4 6 8 10 9 7 5 3 1

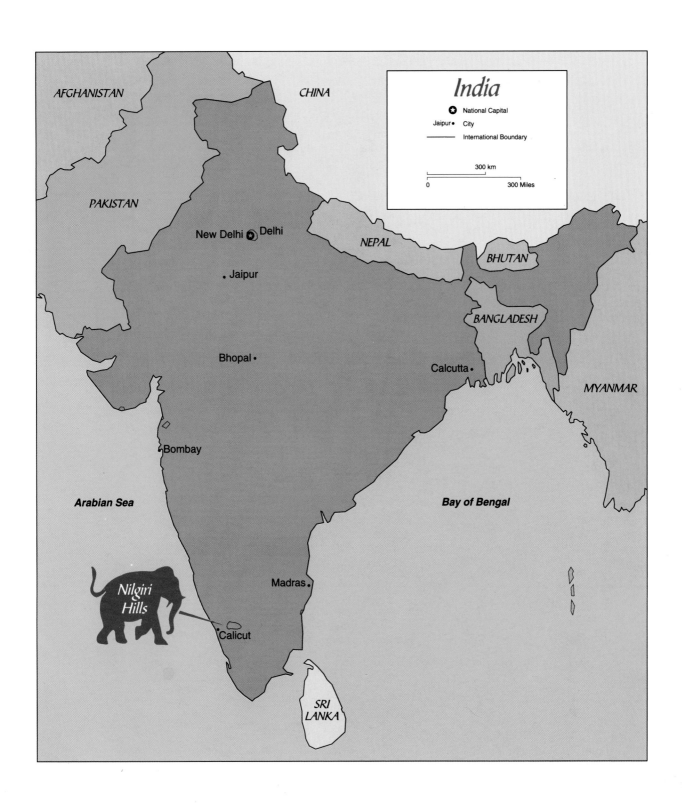

India

National Capital

Jaipur • City

International Boundary

300 km

0   300 Miles

AFGHANISTAN

CHINA

PAKISTAN

New Delhi ⊙ Delhi

NEPAL

BHUTAN

Jaipur

BANGLADESH

Bhopal •

Calcutta •

MYANMAR

Bombay

Arabian Sea

Bay of Bengal

Nilgiri Hills

Madras •

Calicut

SRI LANKA

Having an elephant throw sticks at you might seem like a strange way to wake up, but for Bomman it happens almost every morning. Pieces of bamboo bounce off the wall of his house and fall on the porch where he lies sleeping. He wakes up, but he keeps his eyes closed. He knows it's just his father's elephant, Mudumalai, tossing sticks.

Mudumalai is as reliable as an alarm clock. He spends the night tied to a tree beside the house, and as soon as it gets light, he starts tossing things. They could tie him farther from the house, but Bomman likes having his big friend so close, and he doesn't really mind being awakened this way. It's just that sometimes the wake-up "call" comes too early, especially in winter.

This is February, the season when mornings are cool. During the night, thick fog rises from the river, fills the forest, and settles around the thatch houses of the village. It mixes with the smoke from cooking fires, making everything look soft and mysterious. When Bomman finally rolls over and sits up on the edge of the sleeping porch, he sees Mudumalai looming above him like a great gray mountain half hidden in swirling clouds—a mountain that swings its head, flaps its ears, and has a brass bell around its neck.

With a yawn, Bomman walks over and pats the mountain on the side of his head. The thick, wrinkled skin feels warm in the cold air. Mudumalai swings his trunk back and nuzzles Bomman. The trunk is like a separate animal with a mind of its own, sniffing and blowing, searching for the banana that Bomman sometimes brings in the morning. He has one today, hidden behind his back. Mudumalai finds his banana and eats it in one bite, peel and all.

Bomman and his family live in Abhayaranayam (Ah-bah-*rahn*-yahm), a village in the Nilgiri Hills of southern India. The villagers are Kurambas people, one of many hill tribes that have lived in this region for thousands of years. Once they were hunters who wandered with the seasons. Then, about a hundred years ago, the government realized that the men would make good mahouts, or elephant drivers, because they knew so much about the forest and its creatures—including wild elephants. There is a saying in India that unless you know about wild elephants, you cannot handle tame ones. So the Kurambas men became mahouts. Now they work driving elephants owned by the government. They live in logging camps, moving with their families from one camp to the other wherever they are needed.

Abhayaranayam has fifteen houses, and beside almost every one stands an elephant. There are big males with gleaming white tusks, and several females, one with a newborn calf. The animals live with the people, right in among the houses. At night the mahouts park their

elephants like cars beside their houses, tying them to trees to keep them from wandering off into the forest. Elephants usually sleep standing up, like horses. When they aren't sleeping, they eat piles of bamboo or other food that the mahouts set out for them. Mudumalai usually has something left over to throw at Bomman to wake him up.

Before long, Bomman's mother, Janaki, has breakfast ready—rice, fish from the river, and tea, all cooked on a fire in front of the house. Over the years, many things have changed in this part of India; people have electricity and cars and farm machinery. But the Kurambas prefer their old ways. Bomman's house has a thatch roof, and its walls are made of woven bamboo. It is comfortable and airy, and because the climate is never cold, they don't need heaters. The floor is made of clay. Bomman's mother sweeps it clean and scatters water on it to keep it smooth and hard. This is the traditional Kurambas way.

Bomman is learning to be a mahout like his father. Each morning, he has the same job: to ride Mudumalai down to the river and give him a bath. The first trick is a tall one: An elephant is nine or ten feet high.

How do you get on top? In some countries, mahouts climb an elephant's trunk by grabbing both of the animal's ears for handles and walking up over the forehead. Or the elephants kneel down to make themselves easier to mount. Mudumalai has been trained the Kurambas way. When Bomman says *"Dray!"* Mudumalai holds out his front leg so Bomman can climb it like a ladder, stepping first on the foot, then on the knee. Finally, grabbing the elephant's chain collar, he hauls himself on top.

What a strange place! Because Mudumalai's backbone is too sharp to sit on, Bomman straddles his neck, just behind the flapping ears. To keep from falling off, he tucks his feet under the chain collar. Before doing anything, though, he has to clean off a thick layer of dust that Mudumalai tossed up there with his trunk during the night. He does that to keep insects from biting and also because he just likes putting dirt on himself. Some days, as soon as he's had his bath, he starts covering his back again with mud and dirt. When that happens, Bomman just shakes his head—that's the way elephants are!

"*Hut!*" he says, meaning "Go forward," and Mudumalai moves off toward the river. Although he carries a long stick, Bomman almost never uses it. Most of the time, he controls Mudumalai with words. To make the elephant go, he says "*Hut!*" "Stop" is "*Sayee.*" In all, there are about twenty commands—including "Go forward," "Back up," "Sit down," "Turn around," "Pick that thing up," "Drop it," "Open your mouth," "Push," "Pull," "Stretch out your trunk," and others. Mudumalai started learning those commands when he was a year old. Now he's twenty-seven, and he knows them almost by instinct.

He also knows them by feel. Mahouts can give directions with their feet. For example, to tell Mudumalai to stand up, Bomman rubs his bare toes upward behind the ears. Rubbing downward tells the elephant to sit down. When Bomman pushes with his right foot, Mudumalai turns left, and vice versa. Bomman can use either his voice or his feet, depending on his mood.

This morning Bomman doesn't have to say much of anything at all. Mudumalai loves baths and knows how to get to the river. They walk

right through the village, which is a busy place in the morning. Men are tending the elephants or coming from the forest with bundles of wood. Women are cooking, or washing their babies, or sweeping the ground. With their bells ringing, elephants lumber slowly past the houses while little children play all around them. You might think their parents would worry about the children getting stepped on, but even the smallest toddlers know to stay out of the way when they hear elephant bells.

At the river, Mudumalai wades into the shallow water and kneels down. Then Bomman jumps off and says *"Bai tray,"* the Kurambas words for "Lie down." Mudumalai likes being washed. He rolls onto his side, waves his trunk, and sprays water in the air. With his head mostly under the surface, he can stick out his trunk like a snorkel and breathe.

Bomman could do the job himself, but on most days his father, Maran, joins him, and together they scrub the elephant from the tip of his trunk to the end of his bristly tail. They use chunks of coconut husk for brushes. The skin is warm and knobby, with only a few hairs, and although it feels like tough old leather, it's surprisingly sensitive. Elephants are ticklish. A mahout must always scrub firmly or his elephant gets annoyed and growls.

It's fun to climb around on a huge elephant, but caring for an elephant is a big responsibility. One of the first things Maran ever taught Bomman was how important it is to keep the skin clean. Despite being two to three inches thick in places, elephant skin is easily damaged by sharp sticks and thorns. So while he scrubs, Bomman watches for sore spots, cuts, and infections. Through it all, Mudumalai just lies there happily. He seems like the gentlest animal in the world.

He isn't always. There are times when the life of a mahout is dangerous. All elephants are big and capable of hurting people, even if they don't mean to cause harm. An elephant is especially dangerous during *musth*. This is a condition that occurs mostly in male elephants older than twenty. It happens about once a year—often around the mating season, but Maran says musth and mating don't always go together. Since musth isn't predictable, it is very mysterious and quite scary.

During musth, Mudumalai becomes like a different animal. Instead of his usual gentle self, he becomes aggressive and constantly enraged. He will destroy anything in his path. For two or three months he must be tied to a tree in the forest to keep him from hurting himself or others. No one dares to come within range of his trunk or his feet. Food must be tossed to him. Water buckets have to be set down at the very edge of his trunk's reach.

It is important for Bomman to learn the signs of an elephant about to "turn musth"—for example, oil starts oozing out of two small pores near the eyes, or the elephant acts more stubborn than usual. But sometimes musth happens suddenly, and this is most dangerous because the mahout does not expect it. A few months ago, a mahout was killed while washing his elephant, Subramanian. The mahout didn't know that the elephant was beginning his musth period. While scrubbing Subramanian's head, he touched a sensitive place. Subramanian lashed out with his trunk and threw the man against the riverbank, where he died instantly.

The killing was not intentional, and Subramanian was sad when he realized what he had done. The relationship between a mahout and his elephant is a close one. They are friends—but they have to be careful, or things get out of control.

While Bomman scrubs, the river becomes a busy place. All the village elephants have come down for their baths. There is a lot of splashing and shouting and the sound of scrubbing. Everywhere you

look there are elephants. The biggest one of all is named Anna, a magnificent fellow with huge tusks. He stands nearly a foot taller than Mudumalai, and Mudumalai is no small elephant.

At the same time, walking single file, balancing tall stacks of aluminum cooking pots on their heads, women and girls come down to the riverbank to have their own baths and to wash the dishes. Some of the girls go fishing, using hooks baited with potatoes, or they catch minnows with nets made from pieces of cloth. Because they live with elephants, they know lots about them, but the Kurambas tradition is that only the men and boys actually work with elephants.

"Uttoh!" says Bomman, and Mudumalai stands up, dark and dripping. Pulling water into his trunk, he blows it into his mouth. He does this partly to drink, but also to play. It's like spraying a fire hose in his mouth. Water goes everywhere. Then he decides to be stubborn. *"Saygyo,"* orders Bomman, wanting Mudumalai to turn around, but the

elephant ignores Bomman, or pretends to. *"Saygyo,"* says Bomman, again and again. *"Saygyo, saygyo."* Bomman is patient. He has to be. What else can he do? His father keeps telling him, "You can't force an elephant to do anything. You have to persuade him." After a minute or two, Mudumalai decides he is ready to turn around and lie down on his other side.

In the river nearby is a young elephant calf, only three months old but already big enough to swim. Elephants start out big and just get bigger. Newborns weigh 160 to 200 pounds. This one is over 250 pounds, and almost three feet tall. She is guarded by her mother and her "auntie." When elephants are born, the mother always has the help of another female, the "auntie," who helps look after the baby. In the wild, tigers sometimes try to kill elephant calves. They might succeed were the mother alone, but not if she has help.

A baby usually stays between her guardians—often underneath one of them, when they are standing up. But sometimes, like all babies, elephants forget and wander off. Today, while her mother is lying in the river being scrubbed, this one gets so busy playing in the water that she ends up two hundred yards down the river—by herself. Looking

around, she suddenly realizes she is alone. That frightens her and she yells for help. She has a tremendous voice that sounds like a lion roaring. It's a sound you can't ignore. When they hear it, the mother and auntie go thundering down the river, trumpeting loudly, making water fly everywhere. Only a baby elephant would be comforted by the sight of two huge elephants charging in her direction!

AFTER THE BATH, Bomman and his father take Mudumalai into the forest. For Maran, this is a good way to teach Bomman the skills of a mahout. While his son rides, he walks. That way, he can see how Bomman handles the elephant, and give him lessons.

Winter is the dry season, when many trees and bushes drop their leaves and the grass turns yellow. The parched earth feels hard, like baked clay; the cracks that appear in the ground are big enough to put your hand in. This changes in summer, when the monsoons come: Dark clouds gather, the sky opens, and water pours down night and day until the ground gets soggy and the cracks close. Then the forest explodes with greenery, the perfume of flowers fills the air, and the elephants get their baths straight from the sky.

How different it is in winter, with everything brown and crackly. Maran and Bomman clatter through leaves as dry as giant cornflakes. After a while, they come to a high point overlooking a big valley—a big open valley. There are almost no trees out there, just thorny bushes and dried grass. This was once all forest, until loggers cut the trees down.

Seeing the open space, Bomman has mixed feelings. Logging is what elephants used to do. For over 3,000 years, since the first wild elephants were trained to work for people, logging has been their main job, one for which they are well suited. They like dragging things. By holding thick ropes in their teeth, they can pull big logs. Or they can push logs with their trunks, or lift them on their tusks. A big elephant can move a log weighing more than six tons—heavier than three family cars put together.

As far back as anyone in Bomman's village remembers, the Kurambas people have been elephant loggers. Until just a few years ago, this included Maran. The government owns Mudumalai, but Maran is completely in charge of him, and for them logging was proud work. It took skill and strength and teamwork between man and elephant. But logging ruined almost all of the forest. Too many trees were taken, and not enough new ones were planted.

Logging is now against the law in the Nilgiri Hills (except in tree plantations, which are more like farms than forests). The forest around Bomman's village has become a wildlife sanctuary—no hunting, no farming, no tree-cutting. This is a good thing for the wild animals, including several thousand wild elephants that live in the forest. If the trees were cut, they would have nowhere to go. But for Bomman, it means an uncertain future.

In the old days, a young boy and a young elephant, both around twelve years old, would begin their training at the same time. They would become adults around the time they turned twenty, spend their working lives together, and retire around age fifty-five. One man, one elephant—by the time they were old, they would know each other very well, like a pair of elderly gentlemen. This is how it will be for Maran and Mudumalai someday.

Since Maran and Mudumalai stopped logging, they have done forestry work in the sanctuary. Because the sanctuary is similar to a national park, they are like forest rangers. It's a good job, but one that requires only a small number of elephants, so the government hires only a few new mahouts each year.

Bomman knows that if he wants a job like his father's, he'll need to be very skilled. He'll be competing with other young mahouts who want the same job. Probably he could work on a tree plantation, or go somewhere far away where elephants are still used for logging, but that would mean leaving home and going to places where the traditions are different. He would rather stay at Abhayaranayam, where he'll be close to his family. For this reason he works hard. He needs to be one of the best mahouts.

He has another reason to try hard: If he's really good, he might be assigned to a *koonkie* (*kün-kē*) elephant. A *koonkie* is a tame elephant that helps control wild ones. It takes a particularly brave elephant to do this, and Mudumalai is one of three such elephants in the sanctuary. In fact, Mudumalai is famous for his exploits.

About a year ago, a group of scientists had tranquilized a wild tusker so they could put on a radio transmitter and track him. At first,

the elephant was motionless, unable to move because of the drug. But before the scientists finished, the drug started to wear off. The elephant showed signs of waking up. His trunk started waving. One blow from it could have killed someone. Worse, the tusker was trying to stand up. If he did that, he could trample the scientists. An angry wild elephant is about the most dangerous thing in the forest. But Mudumalai, being a *koonkie*, was not afraid of any wild elephant. At a command from Maran, he turned and sat down on the tusker, pinning him to the ground until the collar was securely fastened.

When they finished, all the people moved back. Only when they had gone a safe distance did Maran say the word for Mudumalai to release the tusker, who by then was fully awake and not happy at all. He jumped up, angry and confused, and ran off into the bush.

Mudumalai's most important work comes in the fall, when fields around the wildlife sanctuary are ready for harvest. That's when wild elephants go outside the forest to raid crops. Naturally the farmers don't like to have their crops eaten by the elephants. They call the forest rangers for help, and the rangers send Mudumalai to herd his wild cousins away from the fields. Sometimes this work ends in a fight. Mudumalai once had a great battle with a wild male. He won—but not before the wild elephant bit off half of Mudumalai's tail! Now he has a crooked stump that isn't much good for swatting flies. But he's as brave as ever.

Turning from the ridge, Maran and Bomman walk farther into the forest. Above them, monkeys leap through the treetops like kites with long, furry tails. Also in the branches are giant Malabar squirrels, as big as foxes. From the forest floor peacocks call, making a high, piercing sound that you can hear for half a mile.

After half an hour of walking, Maran and Bomman come to a stand of bamboo. In this forest, bamboo grows thirty or forty feet high in big clumps that look like tufts of grass. Actually, bamboo is a type of grass, one that grows very tall. Most of the time, Bomman feels gigantic up on top of Mudumalai, but here the high clumps of bamboo make everyone, even the elephants, look small.

Maran climbs the stalks and cuts them down with a machete. On the ground, Bomman trims off the best parts and makes a pile of them until they have enough to fill a pickup truck. But Mudumalai is better than a pickup truck, because he actually picks things up! He slides his tusks under the bamboo, lifts all of it easily, and starts back toward the village. In about two days he will eat the whole pile, and they'll have to come back for more.

The bamboo, though, won't be the only food he gets. Wild elephants feed almost all the time, chewing up hundreds of pounds of grass, leaves, and other plants every day. Working elephants can't take the time to do this, so twice a day they get more concentrated food—a sort of elephant porridge made of rice and whole-wheat flour, and served up steaming hot at a cookhouse in the village.

By the time Maran and Bomman get to the cookhouse, the other elephants have already arrived. They stand like horses at hitching racks, but with a difference: Being so well trained, they don't need to be tied.

Maran measures the right amount of porridge for Mudumalai
(about twenty pounds) and forms it into wads the size of soccer balls.
Bomman then lifts these one at a time to Mudumalai's waiting mouth.
It's quite a feeling, pushing your hand into an elephant's mouth.
Elephants have no front teeth, only big molars. Mudumalai licks
Bomman's hand; his tongue is as big as a watermelon.

All elephants love sweets, and for dessert they get jaggery, which is
like brown sugar. Mudumalai gets two or three chunks, each about the
size of a candy bar. On special days, he also gets bananas.

Morning feedings are a good time for the government veterinarian,
Dr. Bellan, to check the animals for health problems. He goes down
the line looking for cuts, swollen feet, and infections.

The first elephant is moving, swaying his body, swinging his trunk
back and forth. His name is Sandos, which means "Happy." He got the
name because he's always dancing, as if listening to music that only he
can hear. Since he was born he has done this, and he almost never
stops. This morning, Dr. Bellan finds no problem with happy Sandos.

Next is Ravinther, who suffers from an abscessed foot. Abscesses are a common problem with elephants. Being such big, heavy animals, they are susceptible to cuts from stepping on sharp sticks, thorns, and rocks as they move through dense forest. Sometimes infections develop under the punctured skin and are hard to detect until they get large and painful. The mahout must clean the abscess every day. If it gets bad, medicine is given.

The tusker named Subramanian has a different problem, an infection called "sore foot" that makes the foot grow extra skin. Until medicine cures the infection, Masnan, his mahout, must trim the foot every morning. He squats under the elephant's belly, slicing off big chunks of callus with a sharp knife. Subramanian's foot is as big as the man, and much heavier. But Subramanian stands very still, careful not to hurt Masnan. It's amazing to think that this same animal killed his old mahout just a few months ago.

The big tuskers are mature, handsome elephants. When they are all lined up beside each other, they make a big, swaying wall. Someone who doesn't know elephants might have a hard time deciding which one looks best, or which one is strongest. But Bomman, like all the Kurambas people, knows what to look for. He can tell a good elephant the way we can tell a good car or a good bicycle.

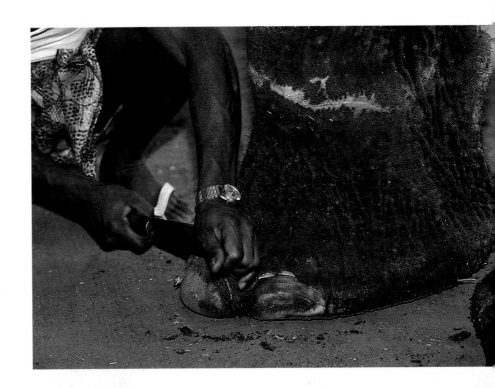

Take Mudumalai. The pink skin on his face is a sign of beauty.
Also, his forehead is broad, which signifies wisdom. And his trunk is
long. When he is standing, it reaches the ground easily, and even coils
back up a little. His tusks are well shaped, curving out and upward.
These are all signs of a good elephant.

Feet are especially important. Mudumalai's feet are big and round,
and he has a total of eighteen toes, five on each front foot, four on each
back foot. A few elephants are born with only sixteen toes, which is not
a good sign; but some have twenty—a sure indicator of strength and
nobility. One interesting thing about elephant size: If you measure
around an elephant's foot and multiply by two, the number you get
equals his height.

Sometimes an elephant has ears so big that they touch in front
when the elephant flaps them. Mudumalai's ears are big, but not that

big. Still, twenty-seven is young for an elephant. He—and his ears—will keep growing for at least ten more years. Elephants flap their ears continually unless they are seriously ill or irritated. So a healthy elephant with motionless ears and blinking eyes is very angry—and dangerous.

In Africa, both male and female elephants have tusks. But among Asian elephants, which live in India, Thailand, and other countries, only the males have them. But not all males. Some have only one tusk, and others, called *makhna*s, have no tusks at all. Female Asian elephants have what are called *tush*es, which resemble small tusks. They are about eight or ten inches long, and are often completely hidden inside the mouth.

The biggest tusks in Abhayaranayam belong to Anna, who is also the biggest elephant. At thirty-eight years old, he is in the prime of his life. He weighs eight tons, and stands nearly ten feet high at the shoulder. He is super strong, an elephant like the ones that ancient kings of India kept for themselves. Such elephants took part in ceremonies, parades, and all sorts of special events. They added dignity to any occasion. They still do.

In India, elephants are a religious symbol. They represent Ganesh, the elephant-headed god who is one of the favorite Hindu deities. No religious celebration is complete without elephants; at really big events, there might be fifty or more of them.

Bomman hopes that one day he can take Mudumalai to a festival. He is sure that Mudumalai, who isn't afraid of wild elephants, would not be afraid of the crowds. He would look splendid, and people would think well of the village from which he came.

But that will happen next year, or maybe the one after. It's something to look forward to. In the meantime, there is more work to be done.

Maran watches Bomman climb onto Mudumalai's back. He isn't worried for the safety of his son. He knows his big friend will be gentle. Elephants and people are very different. But over the centuries they developed a friendship and mutual respect that, in Bomman's village, have not been altered by time or progress.